Mandolin

for beginners

An Easy Beginning Method

Alfred, the leader in educational music publishing,
and the National Guitar Workshop,
one of America's finest guitar schools, have joined
forces to bring you the best, most progressive
educational tools possible. We hope you will enjoy
this book and encourage you to look for
other fine products from Alfred and the
National Guitar Workshop.

Copyright © MMI Alfred Music Publishing Co., Inc.
All rights reserved. Printed in USA.
ISBN-10: 0-7390-1098-0 (Book & CD)
ISBN-13: 978-0-7390-1098-3 (Book & CD)

This book was acquired, edited and produced
by Workshop Arts, Inc., the publishing arm of
the National Guitar Workshop.

Nathaniel Gunod, editor
Gary Tomassetti, music typesetter and assistant editor
Timothy Phelps, interior design and photography
CD recorded at Bar None Studios, Northford, CT

Mandolin photo: Weber Fern Mandolin courtesy of Sound to Earth, Ltd; © Rob Outlaw
Crowd scene photo: © Ken Settle

JIM DALTON

2

Contents

About the Author

Jim Dalton is a multi-instrumentalist, composer and educator. He performs a wide variety of music from classical to jazz, folk, blues and ethnic styles. As a mandolinist, he has played with orchestras, chamber music ensembles, opera and theater groups, blues, jazz, Irish and other bands and has premiered several compositions by contemporary composers. He tours nationally with his wife, Maggi, performing at concerts and festivals and conducting artist residencies.

Mr. Dalton currently teaches at the Boston Conservatory, Indian Hill Music Center in Littleton, MA and at the National Guitar Workshop, where he has taught since 1985. His compositions have been performed throughout the US, Canada and Europe. In 1997, he was awarded first prize in the Toronto Camerata Competition for his choral composition, *The Rocky Road to Dublin*.

Track 1

A compact disc is available for this book. This disc can make learning with this book easier and more enjoyable. This symbol will appear next to every example that is on the CD. Use the CD to help insure that you are capturing the feel of the examples, interpreting the rhythms correctly, and so on. The track numbers below the symbols correspond directly to the example you want to hear. Track 1 will help you tune your mandolin. Have fun!

Introduction

This book is for folks who have either never played music at all or play another instrument, such as the guitar, but have never played the mandolin. It will get you playing right away using tablature, but will eventually teach you to read music in an easy, step-by-step manner.

If you play another instrument already, you may find some of the information in this book to be a review of what you already know. That's okay. Just skim that material and make sure you don't have any gaps. Then keep moving forward.

The mandolin is a remarkably versatile instrument that has been used to play in a variety of musical styles. It is a staple of American, Celtic, Italian and Brazilian folk music. Classical composers such as Johann Hummel and Antonio Vivaldi wrote concerti for it. It appears in operas by Wolfgang Amadeus Mozart and Giuseppe Verdi, symphonies by Gustav Mahler and chamber works by Ludwig Van Beethoven and Arnold Schoenberg. Its sound has graced rock albums by artists such as Rod Stewart and The Hooters, as well as film scores and TV commercials. There is even a revival of mandolin quartets and orchestras—contemporary and classic repertoire for ensembles that first had their heyday nearly a century ago. These are acoustic ensembles of different sized members of the mandolin family, including man- dolins, *mandolas*, *mandocellos*, guitars and bass.

For all its versatility, the mandolin is an easy instrument on which to get started. In this book, we will explore the techniques of playing melodies and chords, which are the basic materials of all the styles mentioned above. We will also develop the skills of note reading and improvisation.

This book assumes you are right handed. If you are a lefty and want to turn the instrument around, simply reverse the instructions regarding the hands.

Most of all, remember to have fun, play your instrument often (alone and with others) and listen to as much mandolin music as possible. Welcome to the world of the mandolin. There is something in it for everyone. Relish the variety.

ACKNOWLEDGEMENTS

Thanks to Dave Smolover, Paula Abate and Nat Gunod for the opportunities that have come my way through the National Guitar Workshop and Workshop Arts. Thanks to my colleagues at the Workshop (especially fellow multi-instrumentalist and mandolinist Seth Austen) for great music and shared ideas. Special thanks and love to my wife and musical partner, Maggi; she is my collaborator, proofreader, sounding board and much more. She has displayed infinite patience through the whole process.

Jim Dalton plays and endorses the Pheonix Neoclassical mandolin made by Luthier Rolfe Gerhardt.

Chapter 1

The Basics

The modern mandolin has four sets of string pairs called *courses*. The strings of each course are tuned in *unison*—that is, both to the same *pitch* (pitch is the highness or lowness of the sound). The back of the instrument can be flat, slightly arched or rounded. The top can be either flat or arched, with either an oval sound hole or "ƒ holes" like a violin. The flat or slightly-arched back is usually preferred by most players of bluegrass, Celtic, blues and other folk or popular music. The shape of the soundholes is a matter of personal preference although most bluegrass players seem to prefer the ƒ holes. Classical players often (but not always) prefer the delicate and bright sound of the round-backed mandolin. None of it is carved in stone. Try many different mandolins and choose the one that suits your taste.

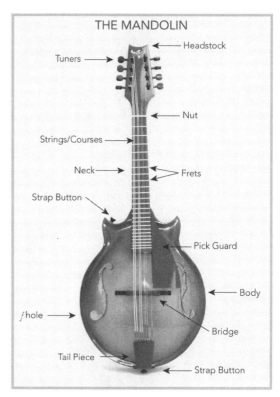

THE MANDOLIN

Headstock
Tuners
Nut
Strings/Courses
Neck
Frets
Strap Button
Pick Guard
Body
ƒ hole
Bridge
Tail Piece
Strap Button

How to Tune the Mandolin

Each musical pitch is given a letter name (see page 10). The mandolin strings are tuned to the following pitches (starting on the 4th course): G – D – A – E. The following instructions will help you tune your mandolin to these pitches. You can also tune to Track 1 on the CD that is available with this book.

Using the tuners, tighten a string to raise its pitch and loosen it to lower the pitch. Always pluck the string and listen as you turn the tuners.

1) Find a source for the pitch of the 4th course (the thickest, lowest sounding pair of strings). This source can be the G below middle C on a piano, the 3rd string of a properly tuned guitar or the G on an electric tuner.

2) Place your finger just behind (to the left of) the 7th fret on the 4th course to sound the pitch D. Match the *open* (unfingered) 3rd course to this pitch.

3) Place your finger on the 7th fret of the 3rd course to sound the pitch A. Match the open 2nd course to this pitch.

4) Place your finger on the 7th fret of the 2nd course to sound the pitch E. Match the open 1st course to this pitch.

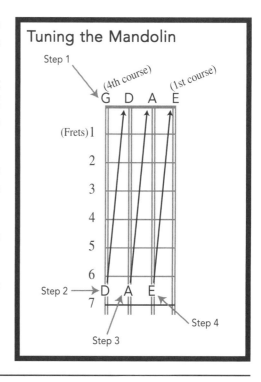

Tuning the Mandolin

Step 1

(4th course) (1st course)
G D A E

(Frets) 1
2
3
4
5
6
Step 2 → D A E
7
Step 4
Step 3

Holding the Mandolin

The mandolin can be played in either a sitting or standing position. The key to success is making sure that the orientation of the instrument (in relation to your body) is precisely the same in either position. This will enable your hands to work in the same way whether you are seated or on your feet.

The body of the mandolin should be at stomach level. The neck should rise from the body with the tuners at or above shoulder level. When you are seated, the instrument should rest in your lap or on one of your legs. When you are standing, it is best to use a strap. If you have trouble achieving the same instrument position when seated as you do standing, you should consider using a strap while seated as well.

Standing   *Seated*

Right-Hand Position

Your right hand and pick are the voice of your mandolin. Proper attention paid to right-hand position at the beginning stage will result in a greater flexibility of technique, and most importantly, a beautiful quality of tone.

Make a relaxed fist with your right hand. *Relaxed* is the operative word here. Try to avoid undue tension in either hand at all times. In the "relaxed fist position," your index finger should be curved to point back toward your wrist and your thumb should lie on top of it. Hold the pick between these two fingers. Your right arm should rest against the edge of the instrument just above the tailpiece. Your wrist should be slightly "arched" or bent inward. You may be tempted to rest one or more fingers on the face of the instrument or to rest your wrist on the bridge—this can cause technical problems for you later. You should fight these urges.

Hold the pick between the index finger and thumb.

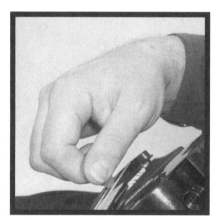

Arch the wrist and curl the fingers.

Picking

Now you are ready to make some sounds. Begin with the pick above the 4th course (ceiling-side). Push the pick toward the floor striking both strings of the course. If you do this correctly, the two strings should sound as one. This is called a *downstroke*. Keep the pick perpendicular to the strings at all times. Play several dozen downstrokes on each course to get comfortable with the stroke and the hand position.

Metronome Markings

You will encounter *metronome* markings in this book. A metronome is an adjustable device that clicks to help musicians find a *tempo* (speed) and keep a steady beat in practice. In a metronome marking, a note value will equal a metronome setting. For example, when you see a metronome marking of ♩ = 92, the *quarter note* (see page 15) ♩ gets one beat and the tempo of the metronome should be set to 92 beats per minute.

Left-Hand Position

The left hand should cradle the neck but not hold it up. Your strap and/or sitting position should keep the neck in position so that your left hand can move freely. The neck should rest in the curve of the hand between the thumb and index finger. Again, remember to avoid tension. If you play guitar, you may find the left-hand position for mandolin to be a bit strange. If you play the violin, however, the position will be more familiar. Two of the main differences between the violin and mandolin are the doubled strings and the frets (violins have single strings and no frets).

Let's get the left hand into the act. Curve your 1st (index) finger over to the 2nd fret of the 4th course and place the tip of the finger just behind (nut side) the 2nd fret. You don't need to push hard; hold the string to the fret so that it can vibrate from the 2nd fret to the bridge. Give the string a good downstroke. If the sound is clear and free of any buzzing or rattling sounds, you've got it. If there is buzzing, or if the sound is muffled, make sure that you are applying enough pressure and that your finger is close enough to, but not on top of, the fret. Try this several dozen times with each finger on different courses at different frets to get a good feel for the way the left hand works.

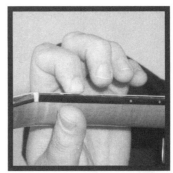

Curve your fingers. Play on the fingertips just on the nut side of the fret.

Left-Hand Finger Warm-up Exercise

Here are the fingers of the left hand and their number names:

Below is a finger exercise to warm up with. You should always warm up before practicing.

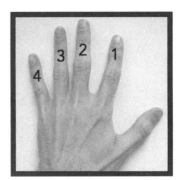

The left-hand finger numbers.

WARM-UP ON THE 4TH COURSE
• Play the open course, then • 1st finger on the 2nd fret, then • 2nd finger on the 4th fret, then • 3rd finger on the 5th fret

As you add each finger, leave the previous finger down on the string in its position while playing the others. Then, lift all three fingers and begin again. Do this four times on each course.

Always pay attention to the quality of the *tone* you coax from your mandolin. Many factors contribute to tone: instrument type, pick, string choice, angle of the pick, left-hand pressure, etc. The most crucial factor is the player's concept of what the tone should be. To develop this ear for tonal quality, you must learn to listen. It may seem almost too simple, but that's all there is to it. Listening to great players will help you to develop a "model" of tone to emulate. You must also listen critically to yourself.

Reading Tablature

Tablature (TAB) is a very old type of notation for fretted string instruments. What it does best is to show which courses to play at which frets to achieve the correct pitches. The four lines represent the four courses of the mandolin with the 1st course on top and the 4th on the bottom. The numbers on those lines designate frets, with zero representing the open course.

It is important to remember that each pitch is given a letter name. The following example shows the pitches G, A and B on the 4th course.

1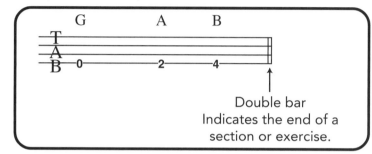

Double bar
Indicates the end of a
section or exercise.

The following two tunes use only G, A and B on the 4th course. Notice the vertical lines in the TAB below. These are called *bar lines*. Bar lines divide the TAB into equal chunks of time called *measures*. The basic unit of time is called a *beat* or *pulse*. Your goal should be to maintain an even pulse. These tunes have four beats in each measure, so you will slowly count "1, 2, 3, 4" as evenly as possible.

The dashes refer to a pause of the same length as the notes. If you can feel a basic, even pulse, and give one pulse to each note and one pulse to each dash, you will play the tune properly.

If you have any doubts, listen to the CD that is available for this book. Play only downstrokes.

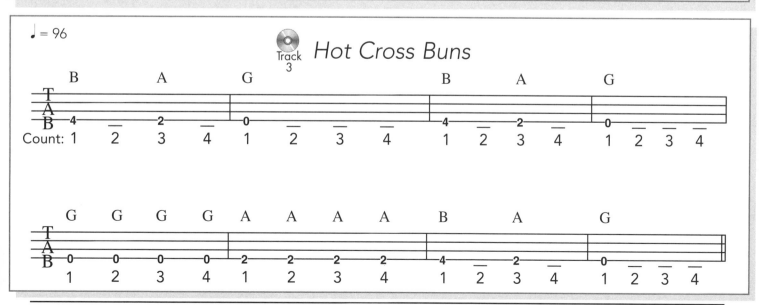

Fingerboard Theory Lesson #1

The pitch relationship from one fret to the next is the same on all four courses, even though each course has a different pitch. Anything that can be played on any single course can be played on any other single course; it will simply sound at a different pitch. To some of you, this will seem obvious, while to others the importance may be obscure; however, this is basic to the logic of the fingerboard, and understanding the fingerboard is essential.

This process can't be rushed, but a little thought and experimentation at each practice session will help the process along. Play both tunes you have already learned on each of the other courses by simply using the same frets as you did for the original. Listen carefully as you play. You will hear the same tune, but on each different course it will sound at a different pitch level.

The Musical Alphabet and Steps

The Musical Alphabet
As you know, each pitch is given a letter name. The letter names we use comprise the *musical alphabet*. This seven-letter alphabet repeats itself many times:

A	B	C	D	E	F	G	A	B	C	etc.

H = Half step
W = Whole step

Steps

We measure the distance between musical pitches in *steps*. The smallest distance between any two pitches on the mandolin is a *half step*, which is the distance between any two adjacent frets. This is true on any course. From the open course to the 1st fret is a half step. From the 1st fret to the 2nd fret is a half step.

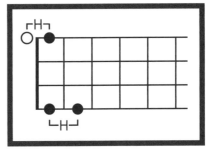

A distance of two half steps is called a *whole step*. From an open course to the 2nd fret is a whole step. From the 1st fret to the 3rd fret is a whole step.

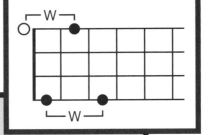

VERY IMPORTANT
There are whole steps between every note of the musical alphabet except between B and C and between E and F.

Understanding the musical alphabet and whole and half steps is fundamental to understanding how your mandolin works. Make sure you understand the material on this page.

In this tune, we add the pitch D at the 7th fret with your 4th finger (pinky). Once you've mastered this tune, play it on each of the other courses as well. Play only downstrokes.

♩ = 96

Track 4 *Merrily We Roll Along*

B	A	G	A	B	B	B		A	A	A		G	D	D	
T
A
B
4	2	0	2	4	4	4		2	2	2		4	7	7	

Count: 1   2   3   4   1   2   3   4   1   2   3   4   1   2   3   4

B	A	G	A	B	B	B		A	A	B	A	G			
T
A
B
4	2	0	2	4	4	4		2	2	4	2	0			

1   2   3   4   1   2   3   4   1   2   3   4   1   2   3   4

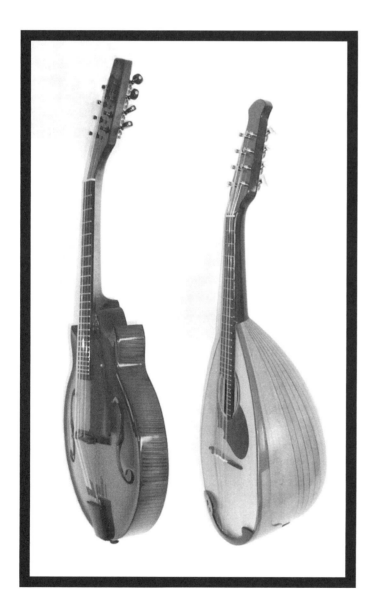

LEFT: *Pheonix Neoclassical flat-back mandolin.*

RIGHT: *Suzuki M-20 round-back mandolin (courtesy of Virginia Kowalski)*

To play *Amazing Grace*, we have to move between two different courses, the 4th and the 3rd. As before, play only downstrokes, keep the pick perpendicular to the strings and maintain a good right-hand position. On the 3rd course, we will play D (open), E (2nd fret) and G (5th fret).

"But wait!" you say, "I have already played both D and G on the 4th course! What gives?" That's right—you played a D on the 7th fret of the 4th course and the open 4th course is a G.

The D on the 7th fret of the 4th course and the D on the open 3rd course are what we call a *unison*. They are simply two different ways to play the same pitch. The G on the 3rd course is one *octave* higher than the G on the 4th course; this means that for the higher G, the strings vibrate at exactly twice the rate of the lower G. (Physics at the service of music.) The two G's sound like the same pitch but in different *ranges*, as if one were sung by a man with a low voice and the other by a woman with a higher voice. They are still both "G." This also accounts for the fact that we only use the seven letters from A to G repeatedly to name our pitches (page 10). See page 13 for more about unisons.

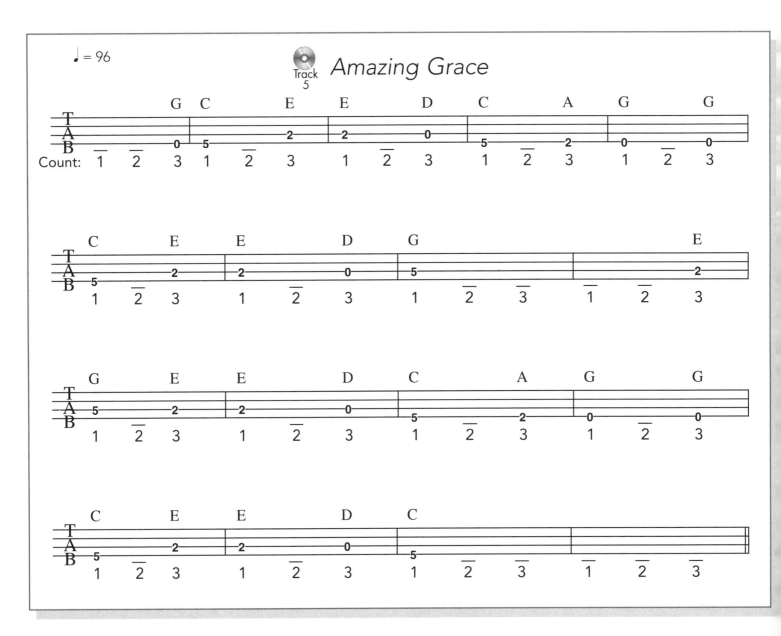

Fingerboard Theory Lesson #2

Place your 4th finger on the 7th fret of the 4th course to sound the pitch D. Compare this sound to the open 3rd course (also D). As you know, the resulting sound is called a unison: the two sounds are the same pitch. (If you don't hear two versions of the same pitch, go back to page 5 or Track 1 of the CD and tune again.)

The same relationship exists between the other adjacent courses:

- The 7th fret, 3rd course and the open 2nd course are unison As.
- The 7th fret, 2nd course and the open 1st course are unison Es.

Try playing these unisons on your mandolin. You can use this knowledge in many ways, such as getting in tune, creating special effects, etc. One way to keep this relationship firmly in mind is to check your tuning every time you pick up the mandolin by assuring yourself that the unisons match.

Since the relationship between adjacent courses is the same, you can play *Amazing Grace* on the 2nd and 3rd courses as well as the 1st and 2nd courses. Try it.

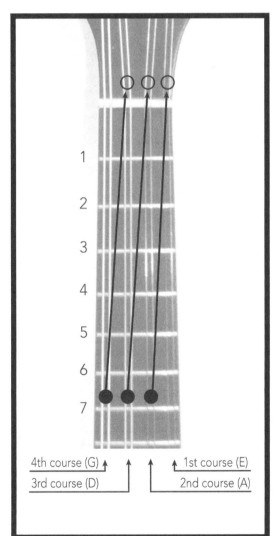

The open 1st, 2nd and 3rd courses are tuned in unison with the 7th frets of the adjacent lower courses.

Chapter 2

Chords are combinations of three or more pitches sounded together. There are many types of chords, some of which will be defined more clearly later in this book.

Strumming

Usually, we play chords by *strumming*. To *strum* is to move the pick quickly across the strings so that they sound together. The motion used for strumming chords with the right hand is just a bigger version of the picking motion. Begin with the pick above the 4th course and lightly but quickly push it through all the courses to just past the 1st course. Again, for the time being we will limit ourselves to downstrokes. Try several downstroke strums before you go on.

Strum down across the strings.

Reading a Chord Diagram

To illustrate what the left hand does to play a chord, we will use another useful notational form: the *chord diagram*. These diagrams show the exact combination of frets and strings required to produce a specific chord.

The figures below will help you learn to read chord diagrams.

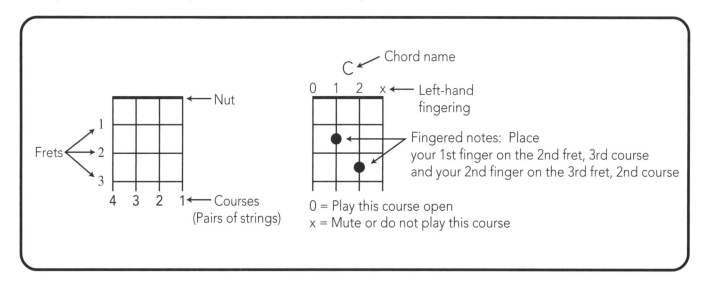

Two Chords: G and D

To play a song, you need to be able to connect the chords smoothly. In the case of your first two chords, G and D (below), there is a *common finger* you can use to slide from one to the other. When starting on the G chord and changing to the D, slide the 2nd finger from the 3rd fret to the 2nd fret of the 1st course while simultaneously moving the 1st finger from the 2nd course to the 4th course. When changing back to the G chord from the D, simply reverse the motion. Do this several times; slowly at first. Then increase the speed of the change gradually, always being sure to move both fingers at the same time. Each chord is shown in the diagrams below. The third diagram shows how the chord change is done.

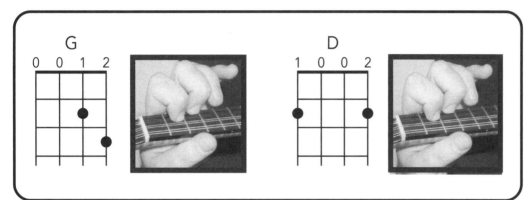

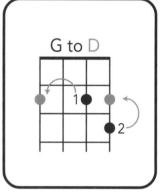

Strumming Chords in Rhythm—Quarter Notes

Rhythm is the organization of music in time using longer and shorter sounds and silences. In standard music notation, *notes* are used to indicate pitches and rhythms. For now, we will use them simply as a way of indicating how many times to strum each chord.

Every note has a *duration* or *value*. This is how long the note lasts.

This is a *quarter note*:

For now, we will consider a quarter note to be a strum of one beat duration. A series of quarter notes will denote strums of equal duration. As with the tablature you learned on page 9, the strums will be divided with bar lines into measures of four beats each. Use all downstrokes for your strums.

In example 2, play four equal strums of the G chord followed by four equal strums of the D chord, then repeat. Be careful not to pause at the bar lines; they serve to group the notes, not to indicate any changes in the rhythm.

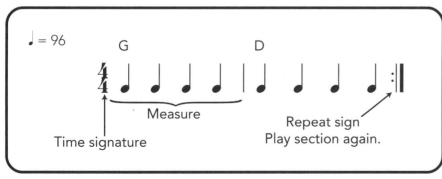

For now, each ♩ represents a downstroke of the last chord indicated until a new chord symbol appears.

16

The C Chord

Let's add another chord, the C chord.

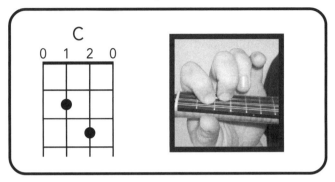

To change from G to C and back, simply lift both fingers simultaneously and move them over one course.

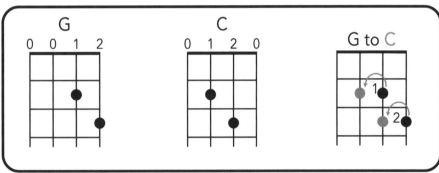

Below is a *progression* (series of chords) with all three chords you've learned so far. Remember, each ♩ represents a downstroke of the last chord indicated until a new chord symbol appears.

3

Track 7

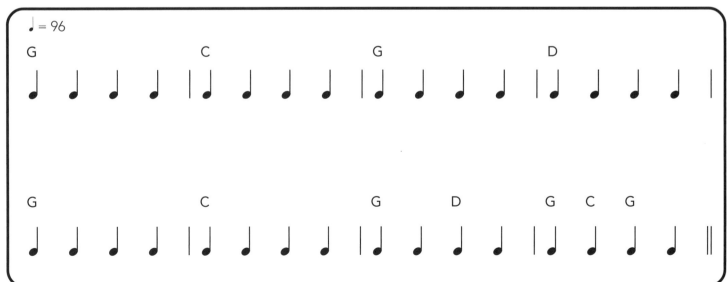

Strumming Chords in Rhythm—Eighth Notes

Let's expand our rhythmic vocabulary by including *eighth notes*. You may have already figured out that eighth notes are half as long as quarters: 1/8 + 1/8 = 1/4. (Don't worry, the math doesn't get any harder than this!)

A single eighth note looks like this:

They are commonly *beamed* together in groups of two or four:

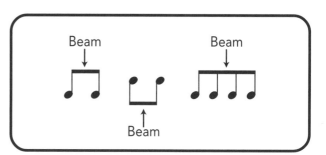

Notice that when you tap your foot as you listen to music, there are two parts to the movement: the part when your foot comes down to the floor (the *on-beat*), and the part when you pick your foot up (the *off-beat*). We have a built-in resource to help us play eighth notes called *alternate picking* or *alternate strumming*. Notice that when you play a series of quarter-note downstrums, your hand moves down for each on-beat and up again in the off-beats. To play eighth notes, simply let the pick contact the strings to perform an upstrum as your hand moves up after every downstrum.

When playing eighth notes, it is important that you count both halves of every beat like this: "1 & 2 & 3 & 4 &." The on-beat is the numbered portion of the beat and the off-beat is the "&."

Here is an exercise for practicing eighth-note strums. Count carefully! Keep your wrist position constant; don't rotate with each strum. Keep the pick perpendicular to the strings. Not only will you avoid undue strain on your wrist, you will greatly improve your tone and projection.

⊓ = Down-strum
V = Up-strum

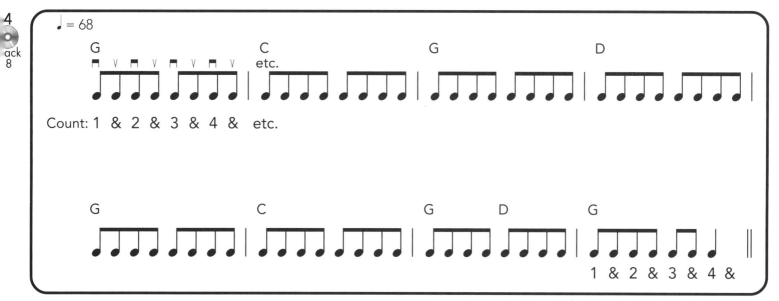

Below are some strumming exercises combining eighth notes and quarter notes.   Count carefully.

o = Whole note. Lasts four beats. (See page 23.)

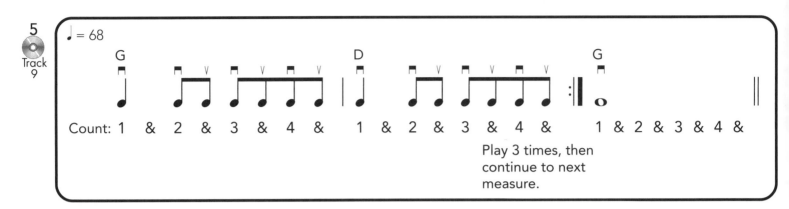

5 Track 9

♩ = 68

Count: 1 & 2 & 3 & 4 &   1 & 2 & 3 & 4 &   1 & 2 & 3 & 4 &

Play 3 times, then continue to next measure.

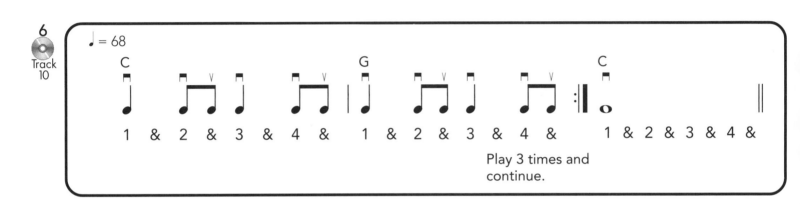

6 Track 10

♩ = 68

1 & 2 & 3 & 4 &   1 & 2 & 3 & 4 &   1 & 2 & 3 & 4 &

Play 3 times and continue.

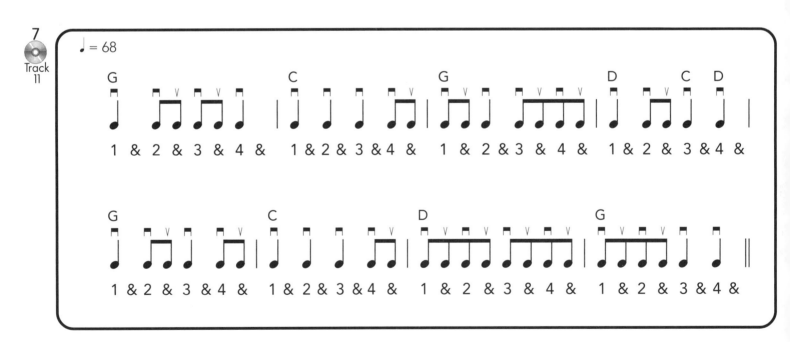

7 Track 11

♩ = 68

1 & 2 & 3 & 4 &   1 & 2 & 3 & 4 &   1 & 2 & 3 & 4 &   1 & 2 & 3 & 4 &

1 & 2 & 3 & 4 &   1 & 2 & 3 & 4 &   1 & 2 & 3 & 4 &   1 & 2 & 3 & 4 &

Three More Chords: A Minor, D Minor and E7

So far, you have learned three chords: G, D and C. These are *major* chords. Major chords are always indicated with just their letter names. In this section, you will learn two different types of chords, a *minor* chord and a *seven* (7) chord.

A minor chord is very similar to a major chord, but the subtle change creates a much different kind of sound. Many musicians would say that major chords sound bright or happy, while minor chords sound dark or sad. In this book, minor chords are indicated with the suffix "min" after the letter name. Here is an A Minor chord (Amin):

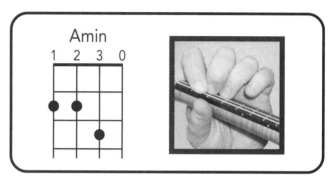

Both major and minor chords are *triads*. That is, they are made with three different notes played together. Seven chords are made with four different notes played together, and the result is a distinctive, bluesy-sounding chord. Seven chords are indicated with the suffix "7" after the letter name. Here is an E7 ("E seven") chord:

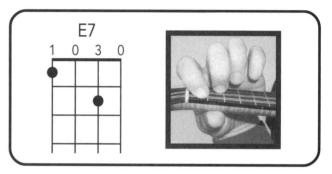

Below is an exercise for practicing Amin and E7. Notice the use of *quarter rests* 𝄽. Use your right hand to stop the vibrations of the strings to create silence for one beat.

𝄽 = Quarter rest.
   One beat of silence.

Here is a D Minor chord:

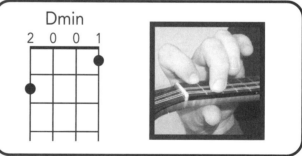

Notice the quarter note rest in examples 8 and 9. This silence is achieved by stopping the vibrating the string with the right hand.

This exercise will give you practice on all three chords, Amin, Dmin and E7. Enjoy!

Chapter 3

Pitch

In the last chapter, you were introduced to reading several note values (quarter, eighth and whole notes), which show when to play and for how long. Pitch notation indicates what pitches are to sound at these times.

The Staff and Clef

A five-line *staff* is used with notes on the lines or in the spaces. As you know, we use only seven letter names for the pitches, and the pitch names repeat in higher or lower ranges.

The notes progress through the musical alphabet on the staff, alternating line-space-line-space. The higher the note appears on the staff, the higher it sounds. So, as we go forward through the alphabet, the pitches get higher.

At the beginning of each staff there is *a clef*. The clef helps us know which pitches are represented by which lines or spaces. The clef used for mandolin music is the *treble clef*, often called the *G clef*. It is called the G clef because it encircles the G line. Any note placed on that line is called "G."

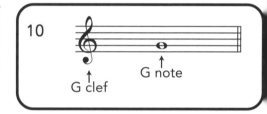

Since we know which line is G, we can use the musical alphabet to figure out the names of the other notes on the staff.

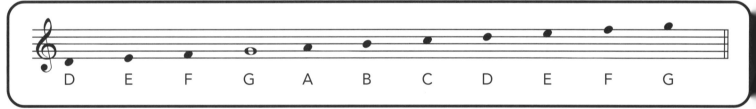

Ledger Lines

To show pitches that are above or below the staff we use *ledger lines*. Ledger lines are short, horizontal lines used to extend a staff either higher or lower.

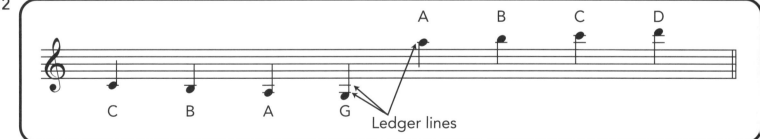

The easiest way to get started reading pitch notation is to learn the symbols for the pitches you have already played. If you memorize just a few notes at a time, the learning will be easy. The example below shows the notes you have already learned plus one new note (F on the 3rd fret of the 3rd course).

13

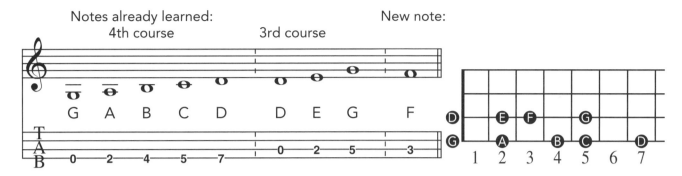

Time Signatures

You learned about beats, bar lines and measures on page 9, and so far, except for *Amazing Grace* on page 12, everything you have played has had four beats per measure. In standard music notation, this is indicated with a *time signature*. A time signature is a sign containing two numbers. The top number tells us how many beats will be in each measure. The bottom number tells us what kind of note will receive one beat. A "**4**" on the bottom indicates that a quarter note gets one beat (four fourths per measure).

4 = Four beats per measure
4 = The quarter note ♩ gets one beat

Read a Tune

You have already played all of the notes for mandolin that are written on ledger lines below the staff, and several that are on the staff as well. In the next example, you'll get a chance to read them and the new note you learned at the top of this page (F). Have fun!

♩ = 96

14

Track 14

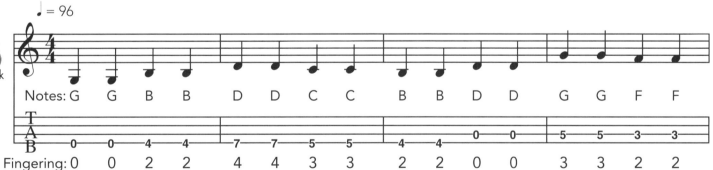

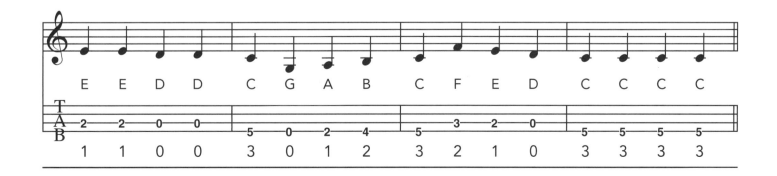

Alternate Picking

On page 17, you learned about alternate strumming (strumming up and down). Alternate (up-and-down) picking is used for single-note playing as well as chords. As you will recall, the first eighth note of a pair (the on-beat) gets the downstroke, and the second (the off-beat) gets the up-stroke.

Remember to keep the pick perpendicular to the strings. Try not to rotate your wrist.

⊓ = Downstroke
∨ = Upstroke

Fingering: 3 3 3 0 0   2 2 2 1 1   3 2 1 0   2 2 0 0 1 1

0 0 0 0 0 0   2 1 1 0 0   1 1 1 1 1 0   1 2 2 4 3

PHOTO • MAUREEN DELGROSSO

Bill Monroe (1911-1996), the "Father of Bluegrass," defined the bluegrass mandolin style for many players who came after him. In addition to his classic solos and great rhythm playing, he was one of America's great songwriters.

Half Notes and Whole Notes

To expand our rhythmic vocabulary still further, we will include the symbols for *half notes* and *whole notes*. A half note is twice as long as a quarter note and a whole note is twice as long as a half note. So, if a quarter note is one beat, a half note is two and a whole note is four. You were first introduced to the whole note on page 18.

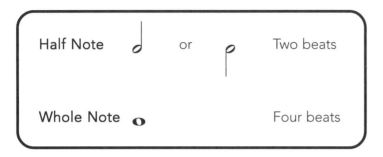

Below is a tune to play using quarter notes, half notes and a whole note. Count "1, 2, 3, 4" evenly throughout.

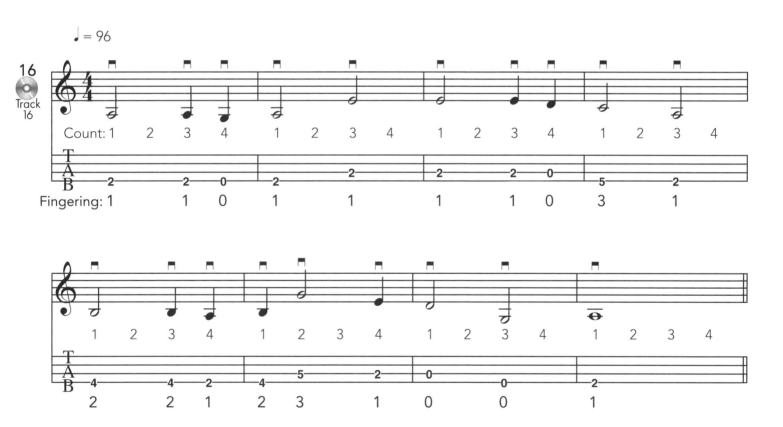

Notes on the 2nd Course

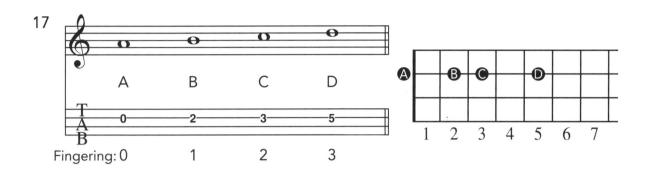

17

Fingering: 0   1   2   3

Here is a tune to play that includes notes on the 2nd course:

♩ = 88

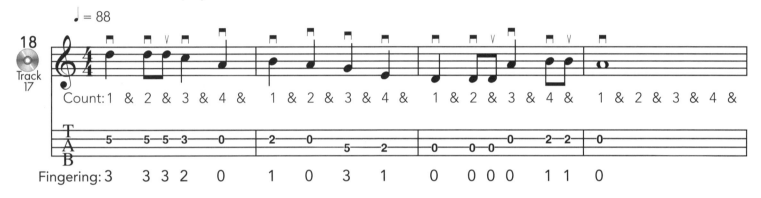

18
Track
17

Fingering: 3   3 3 2   0   1   0   3   1   0   0 0 0   1 1   0

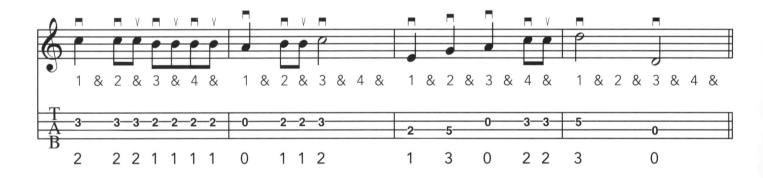

2   2 2 1 1 1 1   0   1 1 2   1   3   0   2 2   3   0

Repeats

Repeat signs are used to indicate that a piece, or a section of a piece, should be played again. You were introduced to the left-facing repeat sign on page 15.

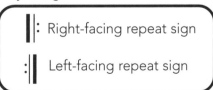

‖: Right-facing repeat sign

:‖ Left-facing repeat sign

The right-facing repeat sign is placed at the beginning of the first measure of the section to be repeated. The left-facing repeat sign is placed at the end of the section to be repeated. If the section to be repeated starts at the beginning of the piece, the right-facing repeat sign is not needed.

Notes on the 1st Course

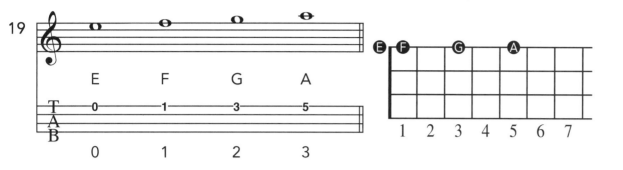

19

E	F	G	A
0	1	3	5
0	1	2	3

Below is a version of a classic American fiddle tune, *Old Joe Clark*. Since the violin and mandolin share the same tuning, much of the violin repertoire lies very neatly under the fingers of mandolinists as well. In fact, the majority of folk and ethnic mandolin music originated with the fiddle.

♩ = 106

Track 18 *Old Joe Clark*

¾ Time

If all music was in ¼ time, things would be boring indeed. As you recall, ¼ time means that there is the equivalent of four quarter notes in each measure; therefore, ¾ time means that you will find the equivalent of three quarter notes in each measure.

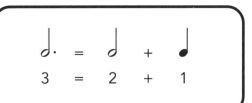

3 = Three beats per measure
4 = The quarter note ♩ gets one beat

Dotted Half Notes

A dot to the right of a note increases the note's value by one half. Since a half note equals two beats, a dotted half note equals three beats (2 + 1 = 3).

Practicing this example will help give you a feeling for ¾ time. In the fifth measure, there are eighth notes on the third beat. It is a good idea to count eighth notes ("1-&, 2-&, 3-&") for that entire measure. That way you'll be ready for the eighth notes on the last beat.

$$\text{♩.} = \text{♩} + \text{♪}$$
$$3 = 2 + 1$$

Below is another tune in ¾ time. You should count eighth notes all the way through this one.

♩ = 88

Count: 1 & 2 & 3 & 1 & 2 & 3 & etc.

Fingering: 0   0 3 2 1 0   0   1 1 3 0 1

1 0 1 2 3 0   1   0   3 0 3 2 1 0

Yank Rachell *(1910-1997) was one of the most prolific and influential blues mandolinists playing both electric and acoustic mandolins. His performing and recording career spanned seven decades and included work as a soloist and with artists such as Sonny Boy Williamson and Sleepy John Estes.*

$\frac{2}{4}$ Time

Now that you can play in both $\frac{4}{4}$ and $\frac{3}{4}$, new time signatures should not pose any great difficulty. In $\frac{2}{4}$ time, there is the equivalent of two quarter notes per measure.

$\frac{2}{4}$ = Two beats per measure
$\frac{2}{4}$ = The quarter note ♩ gets one beat

Here's a tune in $\frac{2}{4}$ you're sure to know:

Track 21 · Yankee Doodle

Here's another tune in 2/4:

♩ = 88

22
Track 22

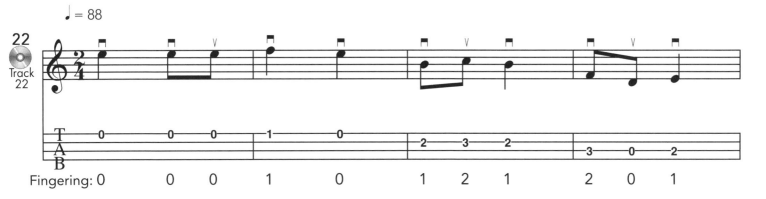

Fingering: 0   0   0   1   0   1   2   1   2   0   1

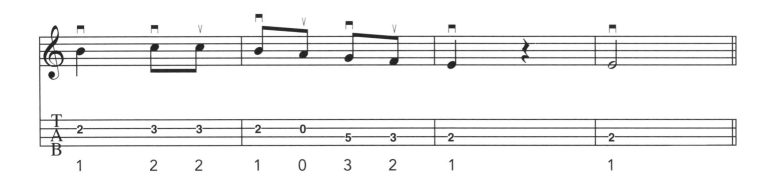

1   2   2   1   0   3   2   1   1

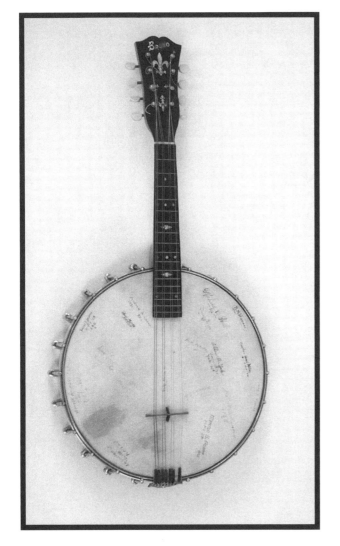

This instrument is called a banjo-mandolin, mandolin-banjo or banjolin. It pairs the neck of a mandolin with the body of a banjo.

Chapter 4

A *tremolo* is a rapidly repeated note. It seems that even from the earliest days of the mandolin, efforts were made to overcome the fast decay and poor sustain of the instrument's tone by using tremolo. The earliest mandolin composers avoided long notes and would certainly never ask a player to make a *crescendo* (gradual increase of loudness) on a single tone; however, when mandolinists played music that was written for the violin or voice, the tremolo was introduced as a way of prolonging the sound and controlling the volume over a longer period of time.

A great tremolo is an asset to any mandolinist's technical arsenal. To achieve a great tremolo takes careful and patient practice. There are refinements to the technique that you should explore as you progress on the instrument, but the basic technique can be understood very easily.

The Basic Technique—Unmeasured Tremolo

As always, relax and keep the pick perpendicular to the strings as you perform the following exercise. Do this for a few minutes every day as part of your warm-up routine.

Track
23

1. To get the basic motion under control, start by fingering a G chord with your left hand. Hold the pick in the usual way—be certain not to anchor your fingers or wrist anywhere on the instrument. Remember that your sole point of contact is your forearm. Now, begin strumming all four courses down and up—not too fast at first—gradually speeding up. Don't play any faster than you can control the motion. This is a tremolo (unmeasured)! Not too hard, is it?

2. When you are comfortable with the four-course tremolo, try using only the two middle courses. This will be a bit harder because the motion must be restricted.

3. When the two-course tremolo is mastered, try a single-course tremolo on the 3rd course.

Obviously, you will eventually want to be comfortable with a tremolo on any one course, any two or three adjacent courses or on all four.

>
>
> When an unmeasured (as fast as you can!) tremolo is called for, the notes will have three slashes on the stem, or in the case of a whole note, above or below the note.

Sixteenth Notes

A sixteenth note is half the value of an eighth note. It takes four sixteenth notes to fill a quarter note value. Sixteenth notes should be counted in a manner that divides each beat into four parts, like this: "1-e-&-ah, 2-e-&-ah, 3-e-&-ah, 4-e-&-ah."

Here is a single sixteenth note:

Consecutive sixteenth notes are double-beamed together.

Measured Tremolo

In order to begin using the tremolo in tunes, we need a refinement. This is called the *measured tremolo* and is indicated by two slashes on the stem, or above or below a whole note. Instead of simply repeating tones rapidly, you will need to control the number of repetitions during any specific note value. This is really much simpler than it sounds. In the standard music notation in the following example, the tremolo is written in two ways (although they will sound the same):

1. The uppermost of the three staves is a shorthand notation that is very common in mandolin music (as well as for other instruments that use tremolo).

2. The middle staff is the written-out version (the bottom staff is the tablature).

Our next piece is a portion of a *Neapolitan* song (from Naples, Italy), *Come Back to Sorrento*. To understand how a song like this should sound, enjoy listening to Luciano Pavarotti sing songs in this style while dining on some great Italian food and then go back to your practicing inspired. Typical of this style, we will only tremolo* the notes that are of a half-note duration or longer. You should practice all tremolo examples with both measured and umeasured tremolos.

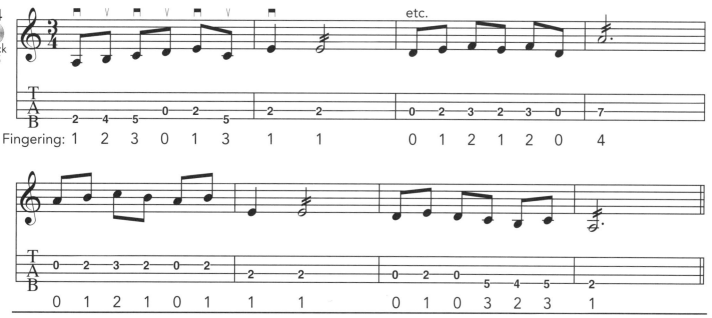

* Notice that tremolo is not typically indicated in the TAB.

Ties

A *tie* is a curved line that joins two or more notes of the same pitch to create a longer note that lasts the value of the combined note values. To most musicians, this means not to articulate (play separately) the second note but simply to continue the sound of the first through the total duration of both tied notes. To a mandolinist playing a tremolo, however, it would also mean to continue an uninterrupted tremolo through the combined durations. Ties can be used to create many rhythms that cannot be written any other way. For example:

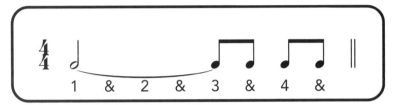

Ties are also a great way to create note durations that reach across the bar line into the next measure:

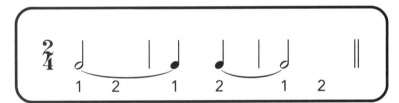

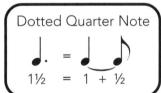

Below is another Italian-style piece. Continue the tremolo uninterrupted through the tied notes. In the sixth measure, you will encounter a *dotted quarter note*, which is the equivalent of a quarter note tied to an eighth note (one-and-a-half beats).

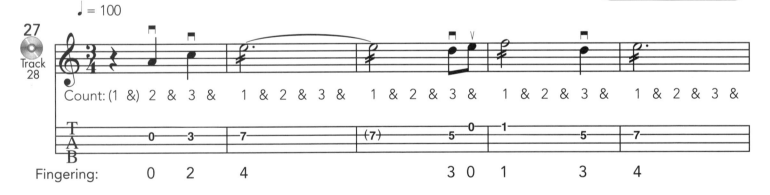

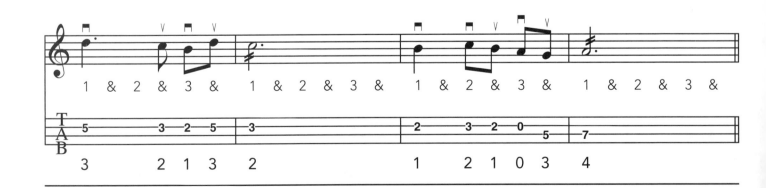

Double Stops

Since you have been playing chords already, *double stops* should be a breeze. The term comes from violin playing. Since a violin has no frets, the strings are "stopped" by the fingers. Playing two tones at once requires "double stopping." The term is used even though we have frets. The notation for this is easy to recognize: Any notes that are aligned vertically on the staff are to be played simultaneously.

In the Foothills is a bluegrass-style piece with some tremolo double stops. You should check out the recordings of the "Father of Bluegrass," the late Bill Monroe. His playing has influenced generations of mandolinists in many styles.

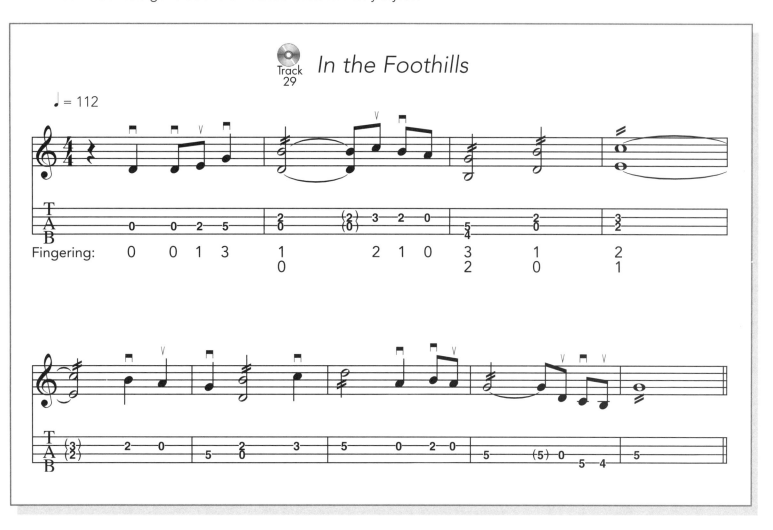

Chapter 5

$\frac{6}{8}$ *Time, Keys and Scales*

The technique of $\frac{6}{8}$ picking is your passport to the land of Irish jigs, Italian tarantellas (see next page) and even the marches of John Philip Sousa. (Yes, during his time, Sousa's marches were often published in arrangements for mandolin and guitar, mandolin ensembles, and even solo mandolin.)

Simple vs. Compound Meter

The *meter* is the pattern of beats on which a piece of music is developed. Up to this point we have only used the so-called *simple meters* of $\frac{4}{4}$, $\frac{3}{4}$ and $\frac{2}{4}$. These are not called simple to imply they are easy. Simple meters allow the beat to be divided into two equal parts (1-&, 2-&, etc.).

28

Compound meters, on the other hand, allow the beat to be divided into three parts (1-&-ah, 2-&-ah, etc.). The easiest of these, and the most common, is $\frac{6}{8}$ time. As you may have already figured out, this means that there are six eighth notes per measure. If we group these three to a beat, we will need to use a dotted quarter note to represent a note of one-beat duration.

29

$\frac{6}{8}$ Picking

The tricky part of all this is the picking. Downstrokes sound stronger than upstrokes (due to the benefits of gravity), so we want downstrokes to fall on the beginning of each beat, which is where the stress should be. Therefore, $\frac{6}{8}$ picking is accomplished as follows:

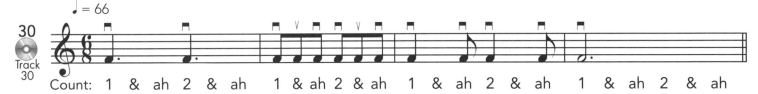

There are exceptions to every rule, including this one. You'll run into them eventually.

Find some $\frac{6}{8}$ music to listen to and count along with. The lively, three-part beat of $\frac{6}{8}$ can be found in Celtic *jigs*, Italian *tarantellas*, much classical music, South and Central American music, and the bagpipe marches of Scotland. For now, find a jig, or the theme music to Monty Python (Sousa's *Liberty Bell March*), and count "1-&-ah, 2-&-ah" as you listen. This will help you get the correct feel. Rhythm is a very physical thing— learn to dance a jig or tarantella. It will greatly improve your rhythmic sense.

The Tarantella

A *tarantella* is a folk dance in §/8 from southern Italy, which folklore says has been used as a cure for the bite of the tarantula. It is usually played fairly quickly with a gradual increase in speed over the many repetitions of the tune.

Track 31 *Tarantella*

♩ = 104

Traditional Italian

* These are *endings*. Play up to the repeat sign in the first ending and go back to the repeat sign near the beginning. The second time through the section, play until the 1st ending, skip it and play the second ending. The same thing happens again in the last two lines except that, when you reach the first ending near the end of the fourth line, go back to the the repeat sign at the beginning of the third line.

The Major Scale

A *scale* is an arrangement of notes in a specific order of whole steps and half steps (review steps on page 10). The *major scale* is a very important scale and is heard in everything from the music of Mozart to Bill Monroe. The arrangement of whole steps (W) and half steps (H) is: W-W-H-W-W-W-H.

Because the musical alphabet has half steps between E and F, and B and C, the C Major scale can be made using only notes from the musical alphabet (see page 10). These notes comprise *the key of C Major*. A major scale starting on any other note, however, will require the use of *accidentals*. An accidental is a sign used to raise or lower the pitch of a note. For example, a *sharp* ♯ raises the pitch of a note by one half step, which is equal to one fret on the mandolin. The F note is on the 3rd fret of the 3rd course, so an F♯ is one fret higher, on the 4th fret, as illustrated in the diagram on the right.

To replicate the sound of a major scale at another pitch level (starting from a pitch other than C) we simply repeat the pattern of whole and half steps. The *G Major scale* (shown below right) requires us to use an F♯.

The note names progress in order from G to G, and F♯ is required to fulfill the whole-step/half-step pattern—a normal F would have made a half step where the pattern requires a whole step. These notes comprise *the key of G Major*.

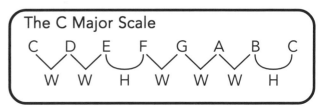

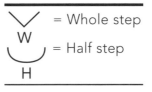

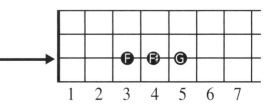

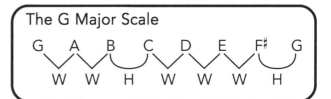

Keys and Tonal Centers

Most music that you will play and listen to in your lifetime will have what we call a "tonal center"—a pitch which sounds like home for the melody, a place of rest.

In example 31, the tonal center is G. The G sounds so clearly like "home" here for several reasons: 1) it is repeated several times; 2) the note one half step below, F♯, acts as a *leading tone*, making us want to hear the G directly afterwards and, perhaps most importantly; 3) the example ends on G. The G is the note upon which the G Major scale is built, and all of the notes in this example are from that scale, making this example in the key of G Major.

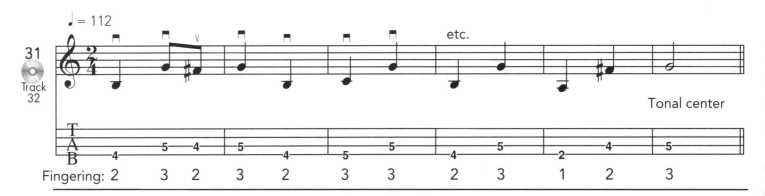

Key Signatures

To make life easier, when writing pieces in this key (and others), the sharp is placed at the beginning of each staff to show that it will be used throughout the piece in every octave (whether it is high or low). This is called the *key signature*.

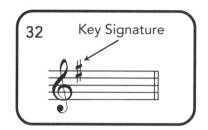

One of the most ancient dance types of Ireland is the *jig*. Jigs are in $\frac{6}{8}$ time. *Kesh Jig* is a very popular jig in the key of G.

Chapter 6

More Tunes

The Red-Haired Boy is an American fiddle tune favored by players of bluegrass, New England *contradance* and other traditional players. It is based on an earlier Celtic tune that still survives as *The Little Beggarman*.

The chords that are included will help you get the rhythmic "chop" of the bluegrass style because they contain no open courses. The first benefit of this is that by releasing the finger pressure (but keeping your fingers on the strings) right after the strum, you create the abrupt, short chord sound that drives the rhythm of bluegrass bands.

Now that you understand the major scale, it is important to note that *chords are derived from scales*. The chords in this song—G, A and D—are all major chords. Major chords are a type of *triad*, which is a three-note chord (meaning there are three *different* notes, although we may use the same note twice in one chord). A major triad is made with the first, third and fifth notes of a major scale. The first note of the major scale becomes the *root* of the chord, the note upon which the chord is built.

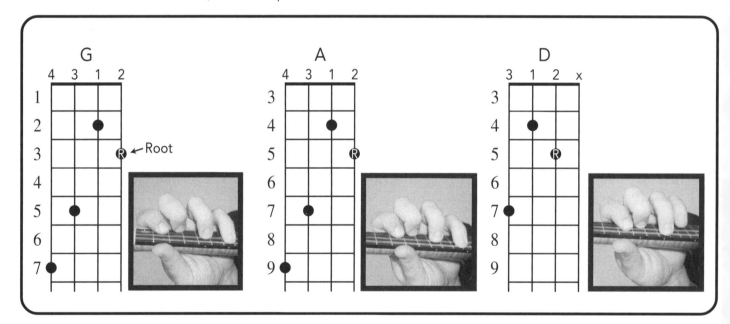

The added benefit of the chords with no open courses is that they are *movable*. Notice the similarities between the G and A chords. They are fingered the same way but the roots are on different frets.

Make sure that you count and strum as follows:

33
Track
34

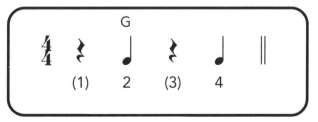

The Red-Haired Boy

♭ = Flat. Lower the note by one half step.

The two preludes that follow demonstrate the technique of *cross-picking*, which is a picking pattern over several strings which imitates a banjo player's *roll* or a guitarist's *broken chord*, thus allowing the tones to ring together. Although this technique has been known to classical mandolinists since the 17th century, bluegrass player Jesse McReynolds introduced it to most contemporary mandolinists. This technique or style of playing has enormous potential. Keep your picking hand relaxed and your pick perpendicular to the strings. Don't anchor your hand, wrist or fingers anywhere. Use strict alternate up-and-down picking.

Notice the flats in the key signature (see page 37).

Prelude in G Minor

Jim Dalton

Track 36

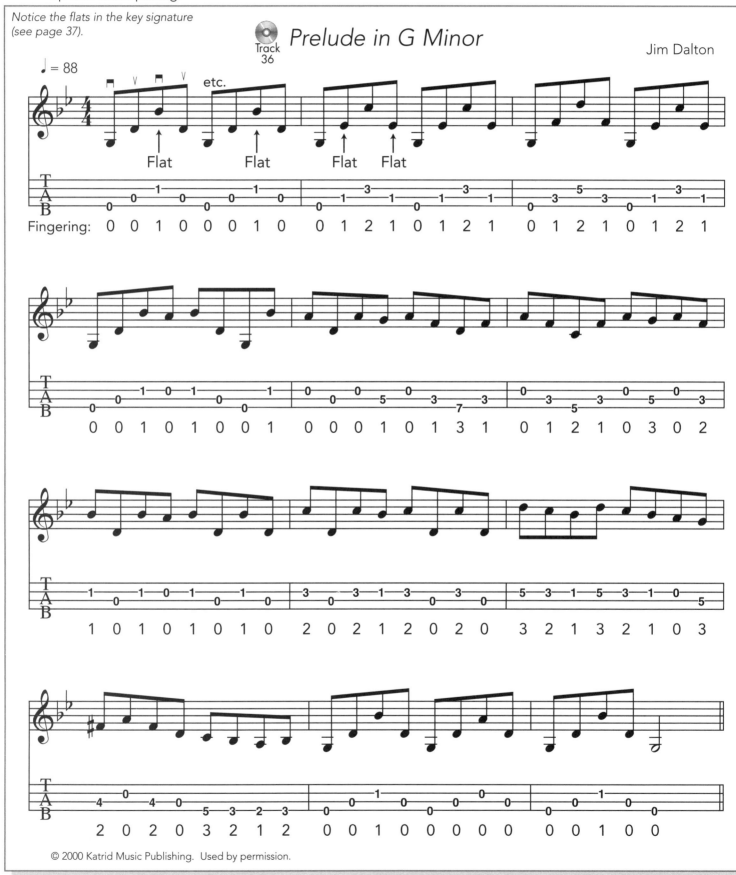

For this next prelude, you will need to learn a new picking pattern. Master this pattern before working on *Litte Prelude in D*.

You will notice that there are new fingerings for many of the pitches. In this case, it is recommended to rely on the tablature over the standard notation so that you get the intended effect.

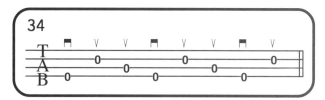

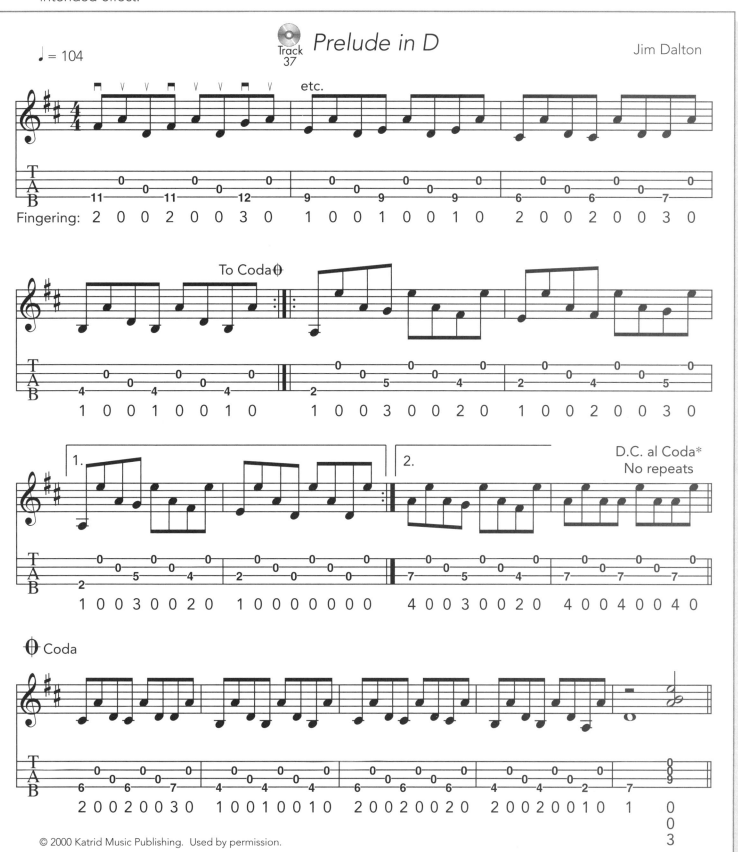

Prelude in D

Jim Dalton

Da Capo al Coda. Go back to the beginning and play again until "To Coda ⊕." Then play the *Coda* (ending section ⊕).

Since the 1970s, the mandolin has periodically been prominently featured on rock recordings by such artists as Rod Stewart, the Grateful Dead, Elton John and the Hooters. This final tune, *Wake Up, Rod*, exemplifies the playing style used by these performers. Use the measured tremolo (see page 31) for this tune.

Wake Up, Rod

Chapter 7

Improvising

Improvising—the spontaneous creating of music—is one of the great joys of music-making. It should be considered a birthright for every musician, at any level of ability, in any style, to create music "where there was none before." It is surprising how many musicians (often even experienced players) don't believe they can do this. We *all* have the most important tools: ears, brains and fingers.

Improvisation can take many forms. It can be anything from a single performer creating a whole piece while playing it; a soloist playing a "break" in a blues, jazz, bluegrass, rock, country, reggae, or pop tune; or a group of musicians responding to each other's sounds in a free, *avant-garde* situation. It can also be a musician creating an accompaniment from chord symbols to his or her own singing, making up a strum that fits the nature of the melody.

There are many highly-developed improvisational styles in the world from India, the Middle East, Africa, America (jazz), Spain (flamenco), etc. All of these require a thorough understanding of the style and its theoretical basis. In fact, for any style, the more experience you have, and the better you understand the musical language, the more eloquently you'll be able to express yourself.

Improvising with the Major Pentatonic Scale

Often, musicians use scales to improvise. The most common scale in the world is the *major pentatonic* scale. *Penta* is the Greek word for "five;" *tonic* is the Greek word for "tones." A pentatonic scale is a scale with five notes.

Let's look at the G Major Pentatonic scale. The notes are G-A-B-D-E. Below is the scale across all four courses, from the lowest G on the mandolin (the open 4th course) up to the G on the first course. The five notes of the scale are marked with brackets.

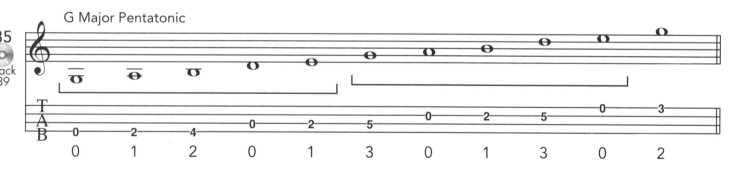

First, familiarize yourself with the G Major Pentatonic scale shown in example 35 by playing it up and down a few times—just to be sure of which pitches to use. Now, play a low G on the 4th course and then play a few notes from the scale on the other three courses while the G rings on. You can't go wrong! Any note you choose from the scale will sound great. For now, just get comfortable with the act of creation.

Example 36 demonstrates a possible improvisation. Notice that the music is written in two parts. The low G (the *bass* part) is played while the improvising part (the *treble*) rests. Then the bass note continues to ring as the treble part continues. In the measures with two parts (1 and 4), the treble part is written with stems up.

Spend a lot of time doing just this. It will build confidence and the beginning of an improvisational vocabulary.

Improvising Over a Chord Progression

A *chord progression* is a series of chords moving from one to the next. For instance, Examples 8 and 9 on page 19 are chord progressions. Look at this chord progression:

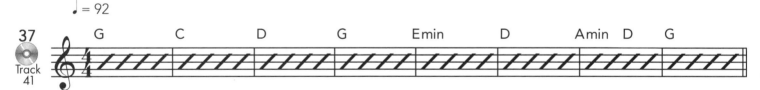

This chord progression is in G Major because all of the notes needed to create all of the chords are found in the G Major scale. Try to improvise over this progression using the G Major Pentatonic scale. You can either record yourself playing the chords (you can strum through using quarter notes) or play along with the CD that is available for this book.

Spend a great deal of time doing this. Vary the note values, add some double stops, some tremolo and so on. In short, try everything you can think of. In this exercise, there is no such thing as making a mistake. Be as creative as you can. Express yourself and have fun.

Improvising with the Minor Pentatonic Scale

The *minor pentatonic scale* is renowned the world over for its usefulness in blues, rock and bluegrass soloing. The G Minor Pentatonic scale uses the following notes: G-Bb-C-D-F. Try improvising with this scale; use it to create a few melodies. It will have a familiar, bluesy sound. The five notes of the scale are marked with brackets in example 38.

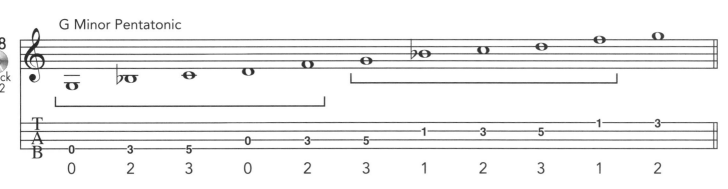

The Blues

The blues originated as an African-American folk music but left its imprint on all American music—and on music worldwide. The clash of African melodies and rhythms with European chord structures created something uniquely American. Fortunately, blues mandolinists such as Howard Armstrong and Yank Rachell have left us models to emulate and be inspired by while learning to get a blues sound on our instrument.

A characteristic blues sound can be achieved by using the minor pentatonic scale over an accompaniment based on chords derived from the major scale (page 38). On page 19, you learned the E7 chord. Hopefully, you noticed its bluesy sound. Here are three more bluesy sounding chords:

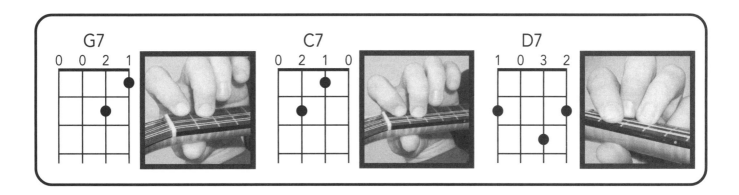

G Blues has a melody that can be the source of some good blues *phrases* (small, complete musical ideas) to use in your improvising. Use the scale to improvise, but occasionally allow your ear to lead you elsewhere...

Well, you've done it. You have gotten yourself a basic technique and understanding of a remarkable and underrated instrument. When the mandolin jokes begin: a) remind the fiddle player that you, at least, have frets; b) tell the guitarist that you have more strings; c) tell the oboe player that you'll have more gigs; d) sneer knowingly at the banjo player. Seriously, though, search out the whole world of mandolin styles, revel in its variety and find yourself a comfortable place in it. Above all, have fun.

Appendix

Chord Dictionary

This handy chord chart should help you navigate your way through hundreds of songs for years to come. Enjoy!

⌒ = Barre. Cover more than one string with same finger.

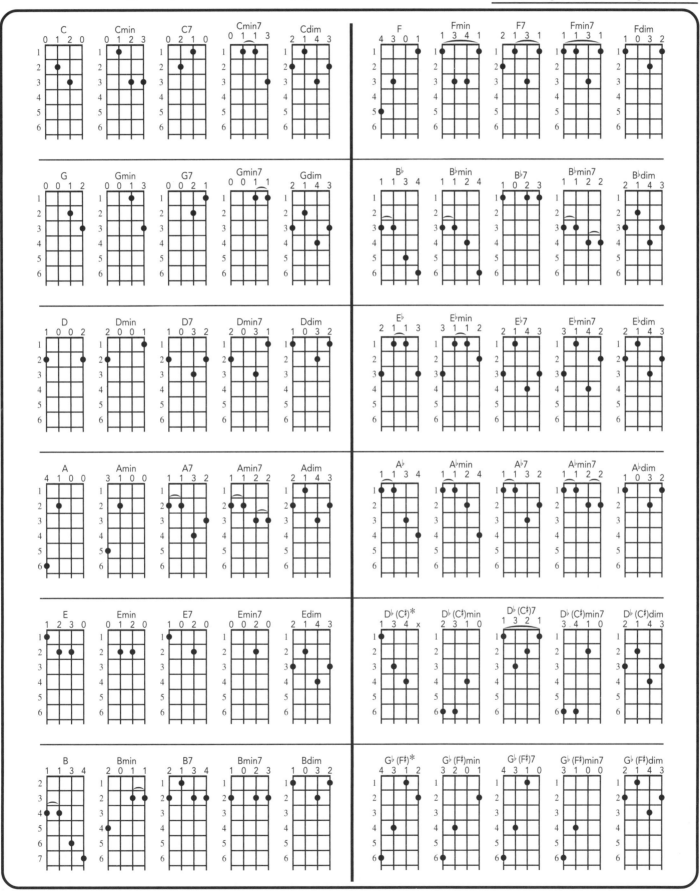

* Mandolin players are more likely to see C♯ than D♭ and F♯ than G♭.

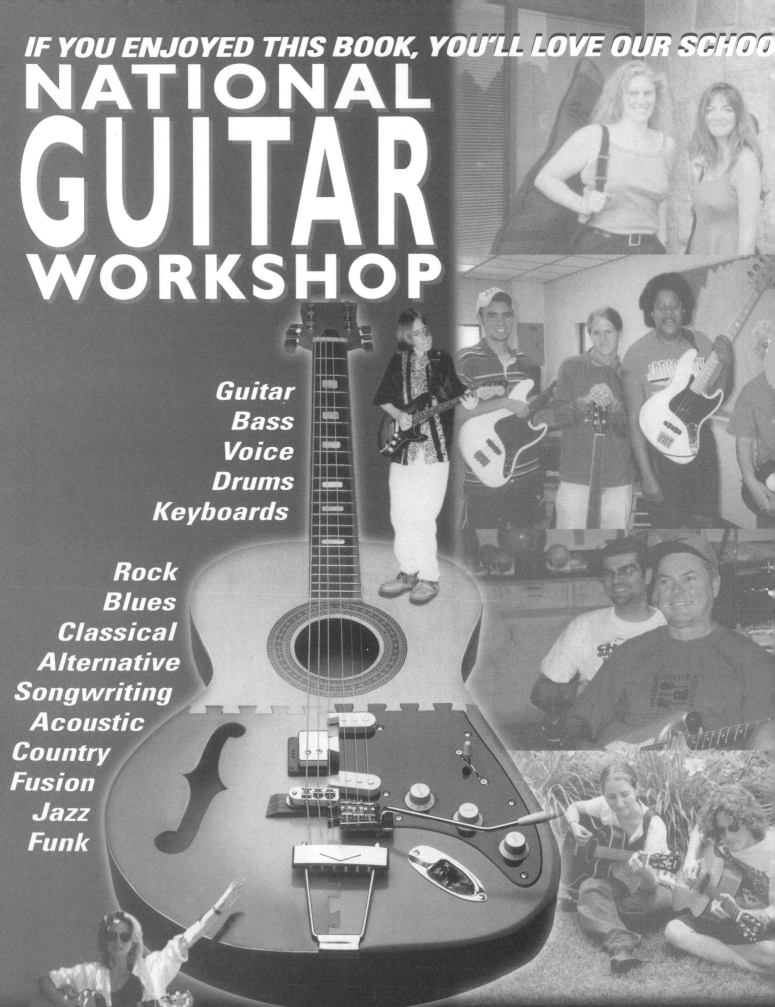